Returning Home:

TAO-CHI'S ALBUM
OF LANDSCAPES
AND FLOWERS

Returning Home

TAO-CHI'S ALBUM OF LANDSCAPES AND FLOWERS

Introduction and commentaries by

WEN FONG

George Braziller
NEW YORK

Published in the United States in 1976
by George Braziller, Inc.
Copyright © 1976 by Wen Fong

Library of Congress Cataloging in Publication Data

Tao-chi, 1641- ca. 1710
  Returning Home.

  1. Tao-chi, 1641- ca. 1710. I. Fong, Wen. II. Title.

ND1049.T3F66   759.951   76-15911
ISBN 0-8076-0827-0

Printed in the United States of America
First Printing

Design by Peter Oldenburg
Map by Joseph Ascherl
Printed by Colorcraft Offset

for Connie

ACKNOWLEDGMENTS

Jean Owen and Adele Westbrook edited
my manuscript; Margaret Setton made valuable
suggestions; I-han Chiang corrected, and refined,
my translations of the poems.
I thank them all warmly.

W.F.

Contents

INTRODUCTION: 13
Mountains and Rivers Remain

COMMENTARIES   36

POEMS AND PAINTINGS   38

COLOPHON   85

NOTES   87

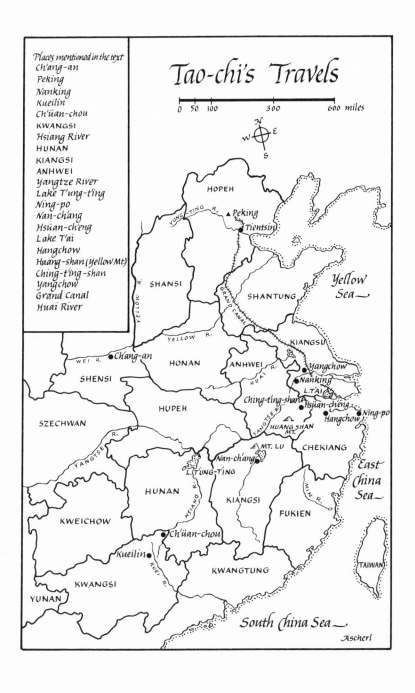

Tao-chi's Travels

Places mentioned in the text
Ch'ang-an
Peking
Nanking
Kueilin
Ch'üan-chou
KWANGSI
Hsiang River
HUNAN
KIANGSI
ANHWEI
Yangtze River
Lake T'ung-t'ing
Ning-po
Nan-ch'ang
Hsüan-ch'eng
Lake T'ai
Hangchow
Huang-shan (Yellow Mt.)
Ching-t'ing-shan
Yangchow
Grand Canal
Huai River

0 50 100   300   600 miles

HOPEH

Peking
Tientsin

SHANSI

SHANTUNG

Yellow Sea

YELLOW R.

GRAND CANAL

YUNG-TING R.

KIANGSU

WEI R.
Ch'ang-an

HONAN

ANHWEI

HUAI R.

Yangchow
Nanking
L. T'AI

SHENSI

HUPEH

Ching-t'ing-shan
Hsüan-ch'eng
Hangchow
Ning-po

YANGTSE R.

HUANG SHAN MT.

SZECHWAN

YANGTSE R.

MT. LU
CHEKIANG

L. TUNG-TING
Nan-ch'ang

East China Sea

HUNAN

HSIANG R.

KIANGSI

FUKIEN

MIN R.

KWEICHOW

Ch'üan-chou

Kueilin

KUEI R.

KWANGTUNG

TAIWAN

KWANGSI

YUNAN

South China Sea

Ascherl

Introduction

> *The nation may topple,*
> *But the mountains and rivers remain.*
>
> TU FU (712–770)

Periods of war and political turmoil in China have also been times of spectacular artistic achievement. Artists who fled to the mountains to escape death and destruction when the T'ang dynasty fell in 906 created the Northern Sung monumental style of landscape painting. And, when all China came under Mongol domination in 1276, scholar-painters, forced into retirement or hermit-like existences, turned to a highly expressive, calligraphic style as a means of "writing ideas" (*hsieh-i*) in painting. Then, in 1644, the Manchus conquered China, and another brilliant age of Chinese painting was born.

The landscapes and flowers of Tao-chi (1641–ca. 1710), a leading artist of the Individualist school of the early Ch'ing (Manchu) period[1] and one who is considered today the most inventive of all the later Chinese painters, exemplify the appearance of sublime poetic and visual expressions in "times of trouble." Such "renaissances" may reflect the Confucian belief in the power of the word, as embodied in the argument contained in the classic *Spring and Autumn Annals:* a scholar may right a wrong and "execute" the wrongdoer with words, or, as the essayist and philos-

13

opher Han Yü (768–824) said, "when injustice occurs, one speaks out" (*pu-p'ing tse-ming*). Thus poets and painters used words and images to bear witness to their fellow citizens, and as testaments to those who would follow.

Art flourished in such times, however, not only as a means of expression but also as a form of psychic self-defense. Since the mid-T'ang period, a pattern of behavior in response to the pressures of foreign conquest had been established: sensitive, intellectual men mourned, reflected upon their personal failings and those of their society, and, in the process, rediscovered the pursuit of truth through art. Their historical knowledge of a man's fate under the yoke of foreign rule made their own experiences of pain, and of mental as well as physical dislocation in the face of this kind of adversity, seem familiar and thus more bearable. Gradually, in their art, a tradition based upon the images and beliefs shared in such circumstances began to take shape.

Tu Fu (712–770), the wandering poet, who saw with his own eyes the brutal devastation of the T'ang capital, Ch'ang-an, during the barbarian General An Lu-shan's rebellion in 756, first established the image of the artist as a lamenting poet:

> The rustic old fellow from Shao-ling weeps with stifled sobs,
> As he walks furtively along the bends of the Serpentine River on a spring day;
> In the palaces by the waterfront the thousands of doors are locked;
> For whom have the fine willows and new rushes displayed their fresh green colors?[2]

Here the artist, the survivor, experiences the tragedy of survival itself: horrors beyond description are taking place while the spring breeze blows fresh and delectable and the fine willows and new rushes sway indifferently, displaying their familiar and innocent charms. Men surrounded by such beauty, but stripped of all rights, face only degradation and savagery at the hands of their conquerors. Tu Fu was almost overwhelmed, yet, as he wrote,

14

"The nation may topple,/ But the mountains and rivers remain."[3]

After the T'ang dynasty fell, Confucian scholars such as Ching Hao (active 900–930), who had retreated to the mountains and rivers that remained, turned to landscape painting as a way of cultivating and expressing a moral standard, and a new image of the artist as philosopher-recluse began to emerge.[4] Under the Mongol conquest a Sung loyalist, Cheng Ssu-Hsiao (active 1240–1310), a recluse-painter and lamenting poet, painted orchids without roots because, he said, "the soil has been swept away by the barbarians"; he carefully locked away his poems of resistance in an iron box which he kept hidden in a dry well.[5]

In 1644, the rebel General Li Tzu-ch'eng captured and sacked Peking, and the last Ming Emperor, Ch'ung-chen, committed suicide to avoid seizure and disgrace. On the pretext of avenging the Emperor, the Manchus occupied Peking and, about a year later, overthrew the Southern Ming court at Nanking. If anything could have blunted the pain of the Ming loyalists' loss, it would have been the similarity of their plight to that of those who had lived under the Mongols more than three centuries earlier. In both crises, martyrdom was believed the most honorable course for key ministers and commanders who had defended the older regimes; others chose suicide as a solution to their personal moral dilemmas. The only remaining alternative was to retreat from the cities and towns, as a form of passive resistance to the new government. Thus while many men died, others withdrew to become recluse-poets or painters.

Tao-chi (also known as Yüan-chi, or Shih-t'ao), the painter and poet whose album is reproduced here in facsimile, was born into a branch of the Ming imperial family on February 7, 1641, in Kueilin, Kwangsi, shortly before the Manchu occupation. In June 1645, his father, Chu Heng-chia, declared himself "Administrator of the Realm" (chien-kuo), but in three months' time his attempt to seize the throne had failed. He was captured and executed by the forces of his rival, a cousin,

15

Prince T'ang of Foochow. Jo-chi (the name the artist was given at birth) was saved by a member of his father's household, who fled with the boy to Ch'üan-chou (Ch'ing-hsiang hsien), at the northern tip of Kwangsi.

When the Manchu forces captured Ch'üan-chou two years later, the young master and his servant took refuge in the priesthood, hiding behind Buddhist names: Jo-chi became Ch'ao-chi, and his faithful companion for the next four decades was known as his "elder brother," Ho-t'ao.

Understandably, Tao-chi maintained a deliberate silence concerning his origins, and accounts of his life by contemporaries are scanty and confused. Only recently has a coherent account emerged.[6] In about 1686, Tao-chi composed a long poem entitled *Song of My Life (Sheng-p'ing heng)*, in which he described his life up until that time in poetic and often vague terms. By interpreting this poem with the help of other records, we can reconstruct the following outline of his biography.

In the early 1650s, Ho-t'ao and Tao-chi left Ch'üan-chou to begin their wandering lives as mendicant monks in search of the Tao (or "Way"). They traveled northeast along the Hsiang River, on foot and by boat, then turned east from northern Hunan into Kiangsi and Anhwei, reaching the heart of the Chiangnan region (south of the Yangtze River). For the next ten years they journeyed all over Chiangnan, stopping at the famous religious shrines and scenic sites. Tao-chi's "Song of My Life" begins:

> All my life I have had noble aspirations
> To renounce this world of dust;
> After enduring war and separation from my family,
> I was confirmed in our true religion.
>
> Seeking the Tao was not an easy journey;
> Even in my dreams, I entrusted my soul to a close friend [Ho-t'ao];
> For thousands of *li* past the Hsiao and Hsiang rivers and Lake
>   T'ung-t'ing,

We traveled on roads that stretched off in the distance toward the lands of the immortals;

Our feet trod the mountain clouds until the clouds dissolved,
Our boat sailed over the stormy dragons which we subdued;
When the five colors of the ocean at last greeted our laughter,
In front of the ever-changing mountain vista, we finally halted.

There was this *Han-pei yüan-tsun* [supreme monument] which shone brilliantly,
I conversed with it at length, when no one else was present;
[Afterward] I turned back, never looked at it again, and went away sobbing,
We had to decide whether to go on to Wu or Chu;

There were many kind voices offering invitations,
And we visited many scenic places;
Like the drifting clouds, once gone, we were gone forever,
Like the ocean waves, we went wherever we happened to land.[7]

A turning point in Tao-chi's life was reached in 1662, when he became a disciple of a well-known Ch'an Buddhist master, Lü-an Pen-yüeh (died 1676). The Buddhist Church, into whose protective embrace Tao-chi and many other refugees from lost regimes fled, was a highly complex organization. Its monasteries offered safe havens for those who, by tonsuring and adopting Buddhist names, effectively surrendered their former identities. At the same time, because of their huge property holdings, individual monastic centers often became powerful political institutions. Leading Ch'an masters competed for well-known recruits: for example, Chi-ch'i of Lin-yen (1605–1672), a leading Loyalist, had among his followers a former prime minister and a former president of the Board of Revenue, both from the court of Prince T'ang.[8]

Chi-ch'i's connection with Prince T'ang's former aides probably meant that Tao-chi, whose father had been executed by Prince T'ang, could not be accepted by Chi-ch'i. (In his long poem, Tao-chi alludes to his painful rejection by a powerful "supreme monument.") In any event, in 1662, Tao-chi became a disciple of Lü-an Pen-yüeh, who was a follower of Chi-ch'i's bitter rival, Mu-ch'en Tao-min (1596–1674).

In 1653, Mu-ch'en, then abbot of the T'ien-t'ung temple in Ning-po, Chekiang, and a fervent Loyalist, published a collection of patriotic poems entitled *Hsin-p'u lu,* or *New Rushes,* a title derived from Tu Fu's famous lines, quoted earlier. Southern Loyalists, highly aroused by this outpouring of sentiment, were cruelly disappointed when the ambitious priest went north to Peking in 1659 to serve the Manchu Emperor, Shun-chih. One man wrote bitterly: "From this day forward we shall no longer cry for the new green rushes,/ We shall leave the flowers and birds at the Coal Hill [site of the Ming Emperor's suicide] to lament alone."[9] Mu-ch'en was accompanied to Peking by Lü-an, who served the Emperor faithfully until Shun-chih died in 1661. It was when Lü-an returned south that Tao-chi became his disciple, and a scion of the Ming family thus joined the collaborationists' camp.

If Tao-chi could have remained near home, as had his distant cousin and fellow monk-painter Chu Ta, also called Pa-ta-shan-jen (1626-ca. 1705), who stayed in the vicinity of Nan-ch'ang, Kiangsi, throughout his life, then kind relatives or fellow townsmen might have helped him. However, a penniless twenty-year-old vagabond priest had no chance of establishing himself except through attachment to a powerful master, and Tao-chi found such a man in Lü-an. Lü-an was an eminent priest, poet, and scholar. It was to him that young Tao-chi probably owed much of his formal education, religious as well as literary. On an important handscroll dated 1667, *The Sixteen Lohans,* Tao-chi proudly signed himself "grandson of T'ien-t'ung Min [Mu-ch'en, Lü-an's master], son of Shan-kuo Yüeh [Lü-an], Shih-t'ao Chi,"[10] and in a poem dated 1689 describing his interview with K'ang-hsi, he was careful to remind this Emperor of his teachers, who had been honored by

18

the Emperor's predecessor.[11] (It is possible he secretly hoped for imperial notice such as that given to Mu-ch'en and Lü-an.)

During the late 1660s and throughout the 1670s Tao-chi remained in the area around Hsüan-ch'eng, Anhwei, living in various temples with Ho-t'ao. In 1680 he moved to Nanking, where his fame as painter and poet grew, and his fortunes improved accordingly. At the Ch'ang-kan (Pao-en) temple, he found his first real home, a tiny structure called *I-chih-an* or *I-chih-ko* ("Pavilion of a Single Plum Branch"). There he and his companion lived contentedly, except for occasional trips, for the next six years.[12]

The events that occurred before his move to Nanking are described in his long poem:

> Near the Five Lakes [Lake T'ai, Kiangsu] where the friendly gulls flew close,
> At the San-mao river [Sung-chiang] there was a holy temple on a high peak,
> In it there was a true priest of the highest religious achievements [Tao-chi notes: "my late master Lü-an"],
> Who had returned from the imperial court to take charge of the holy mountain.

> Three times I faced the examination in the Buddha Hall,
> Repeatedly I was punished, and given a thrashing;
> The master said that I should travel widely to faraway places,
> For to be confined is to become shallow and narrow-minded.
>
> ❦

> In Hangchow we saw the San-chu Temple hemmed in by mountains on three sides,
> We also visited many tall peaks, in misty Yüeh [Chekiang] as well as in moonlight-filled Wu [Kiangsu].
> Just as our friendships with gibbons and cranes began to seem endless,
> We suddenly saw the Yellow Mountain [Hsüan-yüan-t'ai, in Anhwei].

19

The silvery color of the cloud-sea rises up, touching the fragrant mists,

And the clouds carrying the immortals move toward the Peng-lai Island;

We met a prefect who enjoyed whistling through the mountains [Tao-chi notes: "the prefect of Hsin-an, the Honorable Ts'ao Kuan-wu"],

He welcomed us as guests with surprise and delight;

Every day he asked me to write down the poems I composed,

Not a single word was allowed to be lost among the peat and the moss.

How exhilarated I felt in those moments,

Even my garments felt ready to fly away;

Yet, I had hoped to follow Huang-po's way [Ch'an master Hsi-yün, died 850],

So, at Ching-t'ing Mountain, again we lived only with the lonely clouds [Tao-chi notes: "at the old temple grounds of the Ch'an master Huang-po we stayed for more than ten years"].

How tall and difficult to scale were the rocks at Ching-t'ing,

There were two pagodas at the bottom and thousands of trees above;

We rode in the stone-carved boat,

And climbed up the "blue-cloud ladder,"

We laughed out loud at Hsieh Ling-yün [385–433, the poet who first wrote the "blue-cloud ladder"],

"Excuse us, sir, for our careless manners!"

Tiring of our life, we longed to rest,

A friend in Ch'ang-kan [Nanking] promised us a Ch'an refuge [Tao-chi notes "Abbot Chin"];

In a Buddhist haven of golden grounds and pearl trees life should be uneventful.

The solitude of *I-chih* [his pavilion] was just what I needed.[13]

In December 1684, on his first Southern Tour, the Emperor K'ang-hsi paid a ceremonial visit to the Ming imperial mausoleum in Nanking, and Tao-chi—presumably because of his Ming lineage —was granted the honor of an audience with him at the Ch'ang-kan temple. A little over a year later, in 1686 (probably at the suggestion of Po-erh-tu, a wealthy Manchu imperial clansman, intellectual, and connoisseur who had befriended him), Tao-chi decided to go north.

In speculating about the reasons for this decision, two points seem significant. First, in carrying out their conquest, the Man-chus were notably successful in gaining Chinese collaboration. Even before their victory in 1644, the Manchus had organized defecting Chinese troops into armies known as the Chinese Ban-ners; after 1644, they quickly reestablished regular examinations for government service (Mei Ch'ing [1623–1697], a close friend of Tao-chi's in Anhwei and apparently a recluse-painter, stood for a local examination and took a *chü-jen* degree in 1654[14]). In 1679, the Emperor K'ang-hsi established a special examination called *po-hsüeh hung-tz'u,* a name deliberately borrowed from the T'ang period; the examination was to select scholars for work on the official Ming history. Such an enterprise must have tempted even the staunchest Ming Loyalist diehard. The Manchus, however, encountered stubborn and lingering resistance among the southern Chinese, as had the Mongols earlier. Soon after the dangerous Rebellion of the Three Feudatories in the southern provinces was finally quelled, in 1684, the Emperor made the first of his South-ern Tours. Thus the visit to the Ming imperial tombs was specifi-cally designed to mollify the feelings of his Ming subjects. The strategy certainly succeeded in Tao-chi's case.

A second point to remember is that it was no easier then than it is now to earn one's living as a poet or painter. Poetry and painting did give Tao-chi free access to the company, houses, and entertainments of the ruling class, but neither poetry nor painting —and certainly not the priesthood—provided him with a reliable source of income. Throughout his life he led a marginal and often precarious existence: during his prolonged stay in Anhwei

21

from the 1660s to 1680, which was a vital period in the development of his art, he and Ho-t'ao frequently "lived only with the lonely clouds." After moving to Nanking, he finally began to sell his paintings, but his material success was still modest. In a colophon from this period he wrote: "Living in the temple in the summer, the heat was intolerable. Trying to persuade people to give the building a grass shade, I painted this album and waited for a donor. But no one was interested."[15]

Finally, he bade farewell to his Nanking friends in his "Song of My Life":

> Last night I dreamt of going to the capital,
> The [messenger] dove's bell and wild geese were beckoning me;
> An old friend [Po-erh-tu?] wrote me in great detail,
> Asking a southern wind to hasten me northward.
>
> Alas, we are not like wild deer,
>   We neither gather together nor separate lightly,
> Yet all my life I have drifted about, unrestrained,
> I have grown insensitive to the pains of parting,
> And I always listen intently to the pure [friendly] sounds.
>
> My soul has gone ahead to visit the Hua Mountain [in Shensi],
> And I shall not neglect the beauties of the Wu-t'ai [Shansi] and
>   Sung [Honan] mountains,
> I shall travel up the Yangtze and the Huai rivers on my trip,
> And cross the great Yellow River to reach that distant place.
>
> I shall compose my travels into a song,
> And set it to the eight strings [of the *chin*, or zither];
> Let us arrange to meet again in some future year,
> May the river and the city walls witness this promise.[16]

By early 1687, Tao-chi was in Yangchow, Kiangsu, a prosperous metropolis at the intersection of the Yangtze River and the Grand Canal, where wealthy merchants, officials, and scholars indulged themselves in all forms of luxuries and pleasures: works of art, landscaped gardens, theatrical performances, and the company of beautiful courtesans. (One assumes that Ho-t'ao had died by this time, since Tao-chi does not mention him after his stay in Nanking.) In the spring of 1689, after Tao-chi had enjoyed the delights of Yangchow for two years, the Emperor K'ang-hsi honored him with another audience during the second imperial Southern Tour. Perhaps this encounter was the decisive one: at any rate, later in the year Tao-chi began his journey to Peking by boat along the Grand Canal.

Although a priest by circumstances, Tao-chi's talent and ambition drove him on. In 1691, at Peking, he wrote to a friend:

> Half a lifetime, traveling south and north, the traveler's dust has
>   aged me;
> Having renounced the world,
>   I still have many friends in the world;
> I have wandered too long to feel self-pity;
> In the priesthood I rarely find people of my own mind.[17]

In the "floating world" of Peking, he exchanged his poems and paintings for compliments and gifts and joined the ranks of banqueters and party-goers. It was heady and diverting for awhile, but soon his enthusiasm for that life began to wane. In 1692 he was over fifty years old. After a perilous childhood, a lifetime of hardship, and two audiences with the Emperor K'ang-hsi, he was now an artist and poet recognized and praised by the grandees and connoisseurs of the court. Yet he was also profoundly tired and homesick. His Buddhist training merely heightened his awareness of the transitory nature of life and its emptiness. To Mei Ch'ing, his old friend in Anhwei, he wrote:

> How I have spent my years in the yellow dust,
> And white hairs are appearing on my head,
> I am tired. . . . I shall return home. . . .[18]

Preparing to leave Peking in the autumn of 1692, he wrote a poem of farewell to his friends in that city:

23

The K'un-peng [a mythical bird] flies a thousand li,
Unmatched by any other bird;
Yet in the eyes of the universe
Its life is no longer than an insect's. . . .

My own life is like that of an ant,
And I have made many journeys:
Traveling by way of the Chu waters [Hunan],
I came to the Wu hills [Kiangsu];
Finally, riding with the winds along the Huai and Su Rivers,
I sailed here to the imperial capital.

Like orchids *lan* and *hui* we have become close friends,
Like clouds *yin* and *yün* we have mingled together;
I thank you for cleansing my heart of troubles,
And I apologize to you for my unsightly presence.

For three years I did not look back,
But now I must board my boat homeward;
Our good times together will not come again,
So my sorrows shall not end;
With paper and brush I leave you these words,
May our parting sentiments survive a thousand autumns.[19]

Tao-chi returned to Yangchow in late 1692, and his wandering life continued for four more years. In late 1696, he finally built his own retreat, *Ta-ti-t'ang* ("The Great Cleansing Hall"), in Yangchow, and there he remained until his death sometime between 1707 and 1720.[20]

During those final decades of Tao-chi's life, a fortified, if somewhat melancholy man replaced the earlier, restless and vulnerable artist. Even in his Anhwei years, in the late 1670s, he had used a sobriquet, "Hsiao-ch'eng-ko" ("Follower of Hinayana Buddhism"), alluding to his practice of the *lohan* (in Sanskrit, *arhat*) doctrine of seeking enlightenment through personal application and effort; now he began to call himself, mockingly, "Hsia-tsun-che" ("A Blind Arhat")[21] and, still later, "Pan-ko-han" ("Half a Man") and "Tun-ken" ("A Dull-witted Fellow").

In 1696 or early 1697, when he finally built his retreat in Yang-chow, he apparently decided to shed his Buddhist garb altogether. The Ta-ti Mountain near Hangchow, a Taoist center, had been closely associated with certain Southern Sung Loyalist recluses in the Yüan (Mongol) period.[22] *Ta-ti* means "great purity" or "great purification," but Tao-chi placed special emphasis on the word *ti* as a verb, meaning to "purify" or "wash away" all past mistakes and spiritual failings. In a letter to his cousin, Chu Ta, probably written in 1699, he stated emphatically: "Please do not refer to me as a monk, for I am a man who wears a hat and keeps his hair, and who washes away [*ti*] everything in the past."[23]

It is important to recall that Chu Ta, a member of the Ming imperial family (born in 1626), was the famous "lunatic" monk-painter who pretended to be both mute and insane in order to escape the attentions of the Manchu government.[24] He was also a close friend of the Loyalist priest T'an-hsüeh, who died in prison in the 1690s, and who was himself a disciple of Chi-ch'i, the power-ful Loyalist Buddhist master mentioned earlier—and an enemy of Mu-ch'en, Tao-chi's master's master. In an emotional poem to Chu Ta, in 1698, Tao-chi wrote:

> You and I fell ill on the same day,
> Barely born into the world, we found Heaven and Earth quaking;
> You, Pa-ta, are homeless, yet you stay near home,
> I, Ch'ing-hsiang, travel the Four Seas, merely causing my temples to whiten.
>
> On hearing that I am now in Yangchow,
> And have just built the Ta-ti-t'ang near a stream,
> You have kindly sent me a large painting that truly cleanses [*ti*] everything;
> In the blazing, steaming heat of July, it sends forth an autumnal frost.
>
> I read your meaning, yet how do I cleanse everything?
> Your words have rung in my ears through the years of dust and sand;

Because of a single unworthy thought, ten thousand years have
slipped through my fingers,
I can now only wash everything away into a great void, and await
the final crash of thunder.[25]

We can only guess at the depth of Tao-chi's feelings as old age
approached, but he clearly regretted his worldly ambitions, his
connection with Lü-an, the Buddhist master of whom he had
once been so proud, and the signal honor of two imperial audiences. He now dismisses them all as merely consequences of that
"single unworthy thought," and wishes that they could be washed
into "a great void." Although he was fifteen years younger than
Chu Ta, and a child at the time of the Ming debacle—thus
more naturally a Ch'ing (Manchu) than a Ming subject—
according to Confucian tradition he had been born a Ming
prince and must die a Ming Loyalist.

It is interesting to note how, toward the end of his life,
Tao-chi recalled his Ming lineage. There is a seal reading *Tsan-
chih-shih-shih-sun, A-chang* ("a tenth-generation descendant of
[Chu] Tsan-[i] [the second prince of Ching-chiang, reigned 1403–
1408], A-chang [the eldest son]").[26] In his last known extant
works, dated 1707, he used his Ming imperial name, Jo-chi, and
affixed seals reading *Ta-pen-t'ang*, the name of a palace the first
Ming Emperor, Hung-wu, built in Nanking in 1368 for the education of his children.[27]

The album of twenty-four small leaves—twelve paintings of landscapes and flowers and twelve leaves of poetic comments—that is reproduced in this volume was executed in late 1695, when Tao-chi was on his way back to Yangchow after a long trip to Hunan and Anhwei. [28] For four years after he returned from Peking he had been seeking a home: he lamented "my hair is white and I am still without a home."[29] Although his mind was then in a constant state of turmoil, many of his surviving masterpieces date from this period.

Each pair of small leaves in this album is conceived as a single expressive image, with a superb harmony of painting, poetry, and calligraphy. As we turn the leaves a brilliantly orchestrated series of contrasting images appears, in widely diverse moods and styles: the painting is "written" with the same type of brushstrokes as the calligraphy, while in the "painterly" calligraphy, individual characters and brushstrokes, in varying sizes and ink tones, frequently imitate pictorial motifs, such as orchid petals and leaves (Leaf 4), and misty and wavy landscape elements (Leaf 7). The mood or thought in each pair of leaves is described by the poem and then brought to life in the painting and calligraphy—even the painter's seals are precisely integrated into the design.

At first glance, the subjects of these paintings seem conventional enough. Six landscapes and six leaves of flowers alternate. The flowers, arranged according to nature's seasonal cycle, are plum blossoms (Leaf 2) and orchids (Leaf 4) for spring, lotus flowers (Leaf 6) for summer, chrysanthemums (Leaf 8) for autumn, bamboo and dry branches (Leaf 10) and narcissus (Leaf 12) for winter. Tao-chi, however, does not belabor the conventional symbolisms of these themes. In each instance, flower or landscape, the subject is really the painter himself, and the album as a whole deals with life's loneliness and dangers, with love, and, of course, with friendship. The words *han* and *leng,* both meaning "cold," appear seven times in the poems (Leaves 1, 3, 4, 7, 8, 9, 12); *k'u,* or "bitter," appears six times in the poems, signatures, and seals (Leaves 2, 4, 7, 8, 11). *Han-k'u,* life's "cold bitterness," evidently stimulated these beautiful images. The generally emotional tone of the poems gives the paintings in this album a poignancy and a specific referent not usual in Chinese painting: each image recalls a special moment in the painter's experience.

The artist displays a joyous and distinctly sensual feeling for his painted images through magically pulsating brushwork. On Leaf 10, he writes: "I see a beautiful maiden, simple yet elegant, with only a touch of cosmetics." He seems almost compelled to create, an impulse best described in his poem dated in the spring of 1695, when he was visiting Wu-ling in Hunan:

> Near the stream of Wu-ling, brilliant flowers resemble crimson clouds,
> After searching for them in a boat, I feel even more exhilarated;
> Having returned to my hut, I cannot control my emotions,
> So, soaking a brush in the spring rain, I paint my peach blossoms.[30]

How can this frankly sensual love for painted images be reconciled with the painter's Buddhist training, which calls for the extinction of all human passions and desires? A fellow monk-painter, K'un-ts'an (1612–ca. 1686), who was a most rigorous practitioner of Ch'an Buddhism, put it this way: "Painting is my natural vocation. When my ambitions cannot be stilled, I satisfy them through ink and paper."[31] Earlier Ch'an had as its goal the losing of one's self through enlightenment, but since the Sung period, Neo-Confucianism had revived the concept of "selfhood" as the source of human creativity. By Tao-chi's time, Ch'an was richly infused with this Neo-Confucian thought and taught the fortification of one's self: the life of solitude led by these painters freed them from the constraints of aesthetic orthodoxies and established conventions.

In the late 1660s and throughout the 1670s, when Tao-chi was studying Ch'an in temples around Hsüan-ch'eng, near the Yangtze Valley in Anhwei, the reality of life as a poor monk, the cold and hunger, could daunt even the sturdiest mind and soul. He therefore turned to painting for aid in developing self-reliance. In a colophon, probably dated 1679, he wrote:

> Being by nature lazy, and so often ill, I almost felt like burying my brushes and burning my inkstone, since no amount of "carving and skinning" the forms gave me what I wanted. Then quietly, and all by myself, I walked by the Chu-chai [?] studio and saw some original works by Ni Tsan, Huang Kung-wang, Shen Chou, and Tung Ch'i-ch'ang. As my eyes passed over the paintings, my soul followed. For several days afterward, I could sleep well and eat with interest again.[32]

Tao-chi states that he first painted orchids at the age of thirteen or fourteen.[33] This places the beginning of his painting career around 1655, some six or seven years before he became a disciple of Lü-an. In his inscription on the *Sixteen Lohans* handscroll mentioned earlier, Tao-chi's friend Mei Ch'ing identifies the source of his style as Li Kung-lin (1049–ca. 1105): Tao-chi's drawing of both figures and landscape elements follows Li's *pai-miao*, or "blank-outline," manner; his handwriting emulates the archaic "regular" script of Chung Yu (151–230), who was also Li's model.

During the 1670s Tao-chi continued to use his linear, outline-like method. In works dated 1672, 1673, 1678, and 1679, he acknowledged his debt in a seal, *Ch'ien-yu Lung-mien* ("before me there was Lung-mien [Li Kung-lin]"), yet it is doubtful that he had ever seen an original work by that Sung master.[34] By that time (the second half of the seventeenth century), the imitation of ancient masters had become a hotly debated issue. On a painting of the 1660s by K'un-ts'an entitled *Landscape after Mi Fu*, a friend of the artist, Chang I, wrote:

The whole world speaks of poetry, yet how many poets write from their own nature and instinct? The whole world speaks of painting, yet how many painters paint from Heaven and Earth [i.e., nature]? The whole world speaks of Ch'an, yet how many Ch'an masters can throw away the books and smell through their own nostrils? Master K'un-ts'an is a noble dragon, or elephant, among men. Although he is a natural religious leader, he does not assume the usual poses of a preacher; and when he occasionally paints for his own amusement, he naturally attains the highest in that art. In this work, although he claims to have followed the family style of the two Mis, father and son [Mi Fu and Mi Yu-jen], I fear that the Mis could not have equaled him. It is as has been said [by Chang Jung, fifth century], "Do not regret that I have failed to observe some ancient methods, regret only that the ancients failed to observe my methods!"[35]

Tao-chi's linear drawings of the 1660s and 1670s, recalling late-Ming woodblock prints, were executed in a self-taught and exceedingly personal manner. Years later, in an album dated 1694, he wrote: "In this field, those who 'passed through the doors properly' are nothing special."[36] Those who "passed through the doors properly" were painters tutored in the Orthodox tradition, who learned to paint by copying ancient masterpieces according to the methods of these masters. Tao-chi, however, insisted on developing his own method. On Leaf 10 of this album, he mentions Li Ch'eng—the Northern Sung master whose dry branches represented a classical standard—but what he shows there is, instead, a new idea, a "beautiful maiden" with "only a touch of cosmetics." He painted from nature rather than from his memory of former styles.

During the 1680s, Tao-chi began to expand his personal method in calligraphy and painting to a range of related forms.[37] An Orthodox painter like Wang Hui (1630–1717), after imitating a whole range of ancient methods in his earlier years, would eventually try to create his own synthesis.[38] Tao-chi proceeded in the opposite direction, transforming his personal method into a myriad of different forms. In *Hua-yü-lu* ("Notes on Painting"), a mystical tract on painting that Tao-chi composed in the early 1700s, he used the term *i-hua*, which means both "the single stroke" and "the painting of oneness," to describe the creative act, encompassing not only natural phenomena in both a general and specific sense but also the artistic, and art-historical, processes of growth and renewal: the past is alive in the present and the present in the past.[39] He probably based this concept on a conversation between his Ch'an master, Lü-an, and a master Hsiu of the Pao-en Temple in Nanking. As recorded, Hsiu asked, "Take the word one [i.e., a single, horizontal stroke], and add no more strokes to it. What do you have?" Lü-an answered, "The design is complete."[40] The factual answer, of course, is that one plus nothing is still one. But according to Lü-an, this single "one" stroke divides nothing from everything: before "one" nothing existed; after "one" there is creation and civilization, and so "the design is complete." Thus Tao-chi wrote in *Hua-yü-lu*:

> One single stroke is the basis of all things and the root of a myriad of phenomena. . . . When the painter's brush is united with the ink, the cosmic atmosphere [yin-yün] is created. As long as the cosmic atmosphere remains undivided, it is like chaos. In order to bring order to chaos, what else should I use except the "single-stroke painting"? . . . From one comes a myriad of things, and from a myriad of things I must come back to one. By transforming "one single stroke" into the cosmic atmosphere, all things under Heaven may be accomplished.[41]

This theory of *i-hua* or "single-stroke painting" can best be understood through Tao-chi's calligraphy and painting. In works of the 1670s, the "blank-outline" technique constituted, quite literally, his basic "single-stroke" method. After 1680, this insistently linear technique was softened and broadened into a transparent and richly textured brush method.

In this small album, a great variety of methods are consciously employed in the calligraphy and painting: Tao-chi is thus able here to achieve "oneness" through diversity, while creating infinite change through his basic method. In calligraphy, the basic form is the "regular" script (k'ai-shu) in the Chung Yu (151–230) manner, which he renders here in two sizes (Leaves 1, 5, and 8, and 4 and 9); it has square shapes, level horizontals, and smoothly flaring diagonal strokes. The "regular" script of Chung Yu itself evolved out of the more formal and monumental "clerical" script (li-shu) of the Han period (206 B.C.–A.D. 219); this script Tao-chi recreates on Leaf 10 as an ornamental but grave style, with more rigidly controlled verticals and horizontals and flaring diagonals with sharp corners. In a more relaxed mood (Leaves 2 and 6), he executes a combined "clerical" and "regular" script, with slanting horizontals and thinner strokes, recalling the writing style of Ni Tsan (1301–1374). Then, by freely combining "clerical" and "regular" elements in a bold manner, Tao-chi creates an eccentric style that can only be described as his very own (Leaf 12). Finally, by emphasizing certain special features in either brush technique or character formation, or both, he subtly evokes the different manners of such well-known T'ang and Sung calligraphers as Yen Chen-ch'ing (709–785) (Leaf 3), Li Yung (678–747) (Leaf 10), and Huang T'ing-chien (1045–1105) (Leaf 7). Thus Tao-chi, the man who did not adhere to ancient methods, could casually summon ancient styles to his brushtip.

In painting, the basic single stroke of his earlier blank-outline manner is seen on Leaves 6 and 12. The inkwash technique, which sensitively fills out the described form in a single, broader stroke, is best exemplified on Leaf 4. A mixed approach, contrasting the two techniques in various degrees of purity, is seen on Leaves 2, 5, 8, 9, and 10. Finally, in four important landscape compositions (Leaves 1, 3, 7, and 11), the single brushstrokes magically change from lines to surfaces to dots, from thin to thick areas, and from the transparent to the solid, constantly growing and expanding as they crisscross and interpenetrate each other—until suddenly they coalesce into that "cosmic atmosphere" *(yin-yün)* which represents the textures and substances of real landscapes.

In this album we see Tao-chi, a uniquely inventive painter, at the height of his power. His wandering spirit was always seeking to return home, and his wistful odyssey is mirrored here on every page. It is hard to imagine, as we turn these pages, that there was a time when, he sadly noted, "No one was interested."

Commentaries
Poems and Paintings

1

Returning Home

As *falling leaves descend*
with the wind,
I *return by the water*
through a thinning mist;
I *see a tiny hut clinging*
to the bank of a green stream,
How *soft and fat the white*
clouds look in the cold air.

The phrase from which Tao-chi develops his first line is *lo-yeh kuei-ken*, "fallen leaves returning to the tree root," expressing a person's yearning to return home in his old age. The painter perhaps also feels that his life is like *tsan-yen*, in line 2, literally "shredded" or "worn-out" mist. (This album was painted late in 1695, when Tao-chi was on his way back to Yangchow from a visit to Hunan and Anhwei provinces.)

The quality that Tao-chi wanted to capture in this painting is *fei*, the "fat" of *pai-yün-fei* (literally, "white clouds look fat") in line 4 of the poem. Here he appears to reflect the ideas of Kung Hsien (about 1618–1689): "In painting a clouded mountain, the cloud must appear thick [*hou*]. For thirty years I failed to achieve this until I met a master who told me, 'If the mountain is thick, the cloud will look thick. . . . This is the painting of no-painting.' "[42] Tao-chi's misty and wonderfully translucent landscape is composed of two types of brushstrokes: those forming the pine needles and the softly rubbed texture strokes forming the mountain. The "fat" white clouds are merely blank spaces: the illusion of "fatness" is created by the misty forms around them. Tao-chi has transformed his earlier "blank-outline" technique into layers of softly rubbed, transparent brushstrokes. The deep and "fat" quality of the painting results from a subtle intermixing of brushwork and inkwash: different shades of dark and light strokes and textures and solid and void areas interpenetrate one another.

The calligraphy, rendered in Chung Yu's "regular" script, is also smooth and "fat." The round and three-dimensional individual strokes seem to move and twist gently in space, like the falling leaves of the poem. The mood is serenely reflective.

Tao-chi probably cut his own seals.[43] The poem is signed "Shih-t'ao" ("Stone Wave") and is followed by a square intaglio seal, *Shih Yüan-chi yin* ("[disciple of] Sakyamuni Yüan-chi's seal"). The small rectangular intaglio seals on the painting read *Shih-t'ao* and *Yüan-chi*.

諸葉隨風下殘煙
蕩水歸小亭
依琯澗寒觀白雲肥

石濤

2

Plum Blossoms and Bamboo

*First it shows one or
    two blossoms,
Gradually we see five or
    ten flowers;
In a setting sun
    with brilliant clouds glowing
    in the distance,
How the beautiful flowers
    compete with my brush and
    ink.*

During the early Yüan (Mongol) period, scholar-painters developed, as symbols of enduring beauty, the theme of "three friends in winter"—the pine tree, bamboo, and plum blossoms—a theme which also became popular as a decoration for Yüan and Ming blue-and-white ceramic ware. By the seventeenth century, an expanded floral group known as the "four gentlemen"—plum blossoms, orchids, chrysanthemums, and bamboo—had emerged. Here, in an album that requires six floral subjects, Tao-chi adds to the traditional "four gentlemen" two more "gentleman flowers," lotus blossoms (Leaf 6) and narcissus (Leaf 12).

The aesthetic pleasure of planting and observing flowers was reinforced by a well-defined set of moral and spiritual associations which were vital in sustaining the morale of Chinese scholars and artists who found themselves in troubled circumstances. The early

Northern Sung hermit Lin Pu (967–1028), a famous lover of plum blossoms, even fancied himself "betrothed" to the flowering tree. In Nanking in the 1680s, Tao-chi went through an intensive period of seeking out plum trees, while he painted their blossoms and wrote poems about them—learning every mood and nuance of that fragrant flower. In this painted leaf, the ancient, gnarled plum branch, delicately rendered in a dry and light shade of ink, is set off against a crisply executed spray of bamboo in the foreground. A faintly visible inkwash applied to the background makes the plum branch and blossoms stand out as if lightly covered with snow under bright sunlight.

The beauty of the plum painting is so intense that, in Tao-chi's own words, only the real flowers, when enhanced by the setting sun, can compete with it. Cheng Ssu-hsiao, an early fourteenth-century painter who resisted the Mongols, once wrote:

> *For dozens of stubborn years,*
> *I play only with a brush;*
> *My brush is a rootless flower,*
> *Yet every day it produces fruits;*
> *It produces fruits by the thousands and tens of thousands,*
> *Each one shining as brightly as the crimson sun;*
> *Day after day I would pick these fruits,*
> *To offer them as alms to the Buddhas of the Ten Directions.*[44]

The calligraphy here, in Ni Tsan's manner, has thinner and more angular strokes than that of the preceding leaf. The wiry brushstrokes echo those of the painting; the calligraphy even imitates the effect of subtly varying ink tones in the painting: the characters grow thinner as the brush dries and then larger as the brush is reinked. The calligraphy page is signed "Shih-tao-jen" ("Stone, the Taoist"). The oval intaglio seal placed on the signature reads *K'u-kua ho-shang Chi hua-fa* ("painting method of the Monk of Bitter Melon, Chi"). The square seal *Shih Yüan-chi yin*, seen on the preceding calligraphy page, is repeated in the upper right-hand corner of this painting.

初試一桑兩桑漸看十田
五田落日霞明遠映與
余筆墨爭先

3

On the Mountain Peak

*High on the mountain
    the beautiful colors are cold,
Where flying white clouds
    cease to look white.*

On this leaf, the master accomplishes the all but impossible task of suggesting the simultaneous effects of wind, movement, and frigid air, and he does so in an unusual way: in his "flying white" calligraphic technique the ink is dry and thick as if frozen so that the "white" of the paper ceases to "fly" freely through the splitting hairs of the brushstrokes.

For Tao-chi, the ultimate mountain scenery was always represented by the incomparable peaks of Huang-shan, the Yellow Mountain, in Anhwei. By the time he lived there, in the 1660s, he had traveled all over southern China, yet until he saw the massive white clouds moving through the vast "seas" of flowers, trees, jagged cliffs, and blue abysses, he had never felt such infinite space. Here even a life of extreme solitude seemed to have meaning. This group of mountain peaks appears repeatedly in his paintings.[45] As he wrote:

The Yellow Mountain is my teacher,
And I am the Yellow Mountain's friend;
Of nature's myriad different forms,
The Yellow Peaks leave nothing uncovered . . . [46]

The calligraphy here echoes the heroic quality of the mountain peaks: it is executed in a bold and powerful style. The brush with firmly centered tip bores vigorously into the paper in a manner reminiscent of the style of Yen Chen-ch'ing, the famous T'ang master. The calligraphy page is signed "Ch'ing-hsiang tao-jen Chi" ("The Taoist from Ch'ing-hsiang, Chi"), followed by the square intaglio seal *Shih Yüan-chi yin*. In the upper left-hand corner of the painting, there are two square signature seals, *Yüan-chi* (intaglio) and *Shih-t'ao* (relief).

山高萬秀色寒

雲飛不已　清湘道人

4

Orchids

Words from a sympathetic heart
   Are as fragrant as orchids;
Like orchids in feeling,
   They are agreeable and
   always joyous;
You should wear these orchids
   To protect yourself
   from the spring chill;
When the spring winds are
   cold,
Who can say you are safe?

The first two lines are a quotation from *The Book of Changes*. Even in the earliest surviving Chinese literature, orchids are identified as *chün-tzu*, or "virtuous gentlemen." A wild plant that grows in uninhabited mountain valleys, the orchid's fragrance has an aloof and disinterested quality that seems to recall a man of true virtue: it is said that dealing with good and decent people is like entering a room full of orchids; if a person ceases to be aware of the fragrance, it is because he has become such a person. The ancient *Ch'u-tz'u* ("Songs of the South"), on the other hand, speak of how the fragrant and good are often overwhelmed by the foul and evil:

> *Now fragrant and foul are mixed together,*
> *Who, though he labored all night, could discern between them?*
> *Why have the sweet flowers died so soon?*
> *A light frost descended and mowed them all down.*[47]

Under the Mongols, Cheng Ssu-hsiao (who painted orchids without roots because his "soil had been swept away") once executed a long ink handscroll of orchids, and remarked: "All of them are virtuous gentlemen; no mean-spirited people are allowed!"[48] Tao-chi, however, held a more generous, and more realistic, view of the world. In his painting, the lovely orchids are shown with two thorny branches—the latter representing the brambles, or "stinking weeds," decried in the *Ch'u-tz'u*—indicating that in nature the bad is found, and must be accepted, together with the good. In this painting the orchids, symbols of friendship between virtuous men, present almost smiling, welcoming countenances. Only the last line of the poem reminds us of Tao-chi's ever-present sense of living in precarious times.

The calligraphy of the poem (in the Chung Yu manner), with its softly undulating strokes and gently rising and fading ink tones, simulates the swaying orchid leaves and blossoms. The poem is signed "K'u-kua lao-jen Chi" ("Old Man of Bitter Melon, Chi"). The signature is followed by a rectangular intaglio seal, *Ch'ien-yu Lung-mien Chi* ("before me there was [Li] Lung-mien"). The painting bears the double name seals *Yüan-chi* and *Shih-t'ao*.

同心之言其臭如蘭如蘭之熏

其合永歡子宜佩之保護

春寒春風寒兮誰謂乎

安

苦瓜老人濟

5

A Despondent Man from Ch'ing-Hsiang

A *despondent man from*
  Ch'ing-hsiang
Passes by looking
  for old friends;
With no money to buy
  a mountain to live on,
He sleeps peacefully, pillowing
  his head on his own fist;
Though he has seen much,
  beyond many rivers and skies,
He loses his heart to
  the Ts'un-ts'ao-t'ing
  ["Inch-sized Thatched Hut"];
In a light skiff you and he
  toured together,
Not even a boatman was present
  to distract you.

In early 1695, Tao-chi visited Wu-ling in Hunan province—the famous "Peach Blossom Land" of T'ao Ch'ien (365–427).[49] On his journey home, he found himself in the Yangtze River village of Pai-sha (Pai-sha chiang-ts'un), south of I-cheng, on the northern shore of the river, near Yangchow. There, he visited many famous sights in the company of the calligrapher-poet Hsien Chu and others, and wrote many poems.[50]

This poem was written right after he arrived at Pai-sha: originally line 2 read "stops by looking for old friends." The poem seems to have been addressed to the owner of the "Inch-sized Thatched Hut"; Tao-chi was seeking—in fact, begging for—a place to settle down, but it was not to be. In a note following the poem on this leaf, he explains that he is changing the word *t'ing* ("stops") to *ko* ("passes") because he is on a boat, ready to leave Pai-sha.

Tao-chi often represents himself in a skiff in his paintings, and this is one of the most vivid such presentations. While the poem and the calligraphy reveal the author's heavy heart, the drawing is simple and airy—just another journey, aided by a strong wind. The distant mountains and reeds on the river shores recede swiftly as the man in the boat, the ribbons on his hat flapping in the wind, is swept onward.

The calligraphy in the Chung Yu manner, filling the page, contrasts nicely with the painting's sparseness. The poem is signed "Chih-hsia-jen Chi" ("man under the single plum branch, Chi," a reference to his old Nanking residence, I-chih-ko); the signature is followed by the square intaglio seal *Shih Yüan-chi yin*. In the upper right-hand corner of the painting are the double name seals *Yüan-chi* and *Shih-t'ao*.

Visible, in the space below the boat, is the stain of a seal smudged accidentally on the back of the painting.

潦倒清湘客因尋故藿舊過

買山無力住就擔宿奉寧

放眼江天外縣心寸艸亭扁舟

偕子顧布且不算丁　傅書之囑　登舟故肩

白雪江柳當別　橤下人溶

6

Gathering Lotus Flowers

Fields of flowers and leaves fill
Ditches full of water,
A fragrant breeze lingers
By a boat gathering
lotus flowers;
Phrases of a tune mixed
with the sound of oars
striking the water,
Stir the white clouds,
Setting bits of them afloat.

This poem was also written while the painter was visiting the village of Pai-sha. The lotus flower was also thought to possess "gentlemanly" qualities because, in the words of Chou Tun-i (1017–1073), "How spotlessly it arises from its slimy bed! How modestly it reposes on the surface of the clear pool!"[51] While at Pai-sha, Tao-chi went boating with friends in waters full of lotus flowers. The painting supports the lyrical mood of the poem —the shapes of the lotus leaves and petals look like drifting skiffs and floating clouds, and the swaying reeds suggest the movement of "oars striking the water." A heady and unmistakable fragrance seems to emanate from the center of the page, where a large pod, bursting with ripe seeds surrounded by stamens, looks like a giant powder puff.

Technically, the painting is remarkably simple: delicate line drawings in the "blank-outline" style, occasionally reinforced with darker ink for accent, combine with inkwash applied in intaglio style, the whole suddenly bringing forms into three-dimensional relief. There seems to be a deliberate interplay between the painting and the seals in its upper right-hand corner: the intaglio and relief patterns of the seals are echoed by the contrasting "blank-outlined" (positive, or relief) and inkwashed (negative, or intaglio) areas of the rolled-up leaf in the foreground. Without color (except for the vermilion of the seals), the painting seems to throb with life, and actually *feels* colorful.

The calligraphy, in a free Ni Tsan manner, is also lyrical in its movements, with fluent and occasionally circular strokes evoking floating clouds and "oars striking the water." The poem is signed "Hsia-tsun-che Chi" ("the blind arhat, Chi"), and is followed by the same pair of name seals, *Yüan-chi* and *Shih-t'ao*.

花葉田々水滿溝香風
唼喋採蓮舟一餉歟韻
一聲鷗鷺起空翠戲片
浮

白沙江邨採蓮舟中寫
意　曉葊書浮

7

The Wilderness Hut

A wilderness hut,
lonely and desolate,
On a wild mountainside,
A flowerless old tree
Leaning over
the water's edge;
After supper, I wander here
Seeking quiet scenery,
How sad the sunset feels,
When I am so cold
and bitter.

This poem and painting give a picture of the hermit's hard and lonely existence, which Tao-chi well knew. In a poem dated 1674, Mei Ch'ing described the life of Tao-chi and Ho-t'ao on the Ching-t'ing mountain in Anhwei: "The cold wind regularly blows through their thatch-covered walls; when the last scraps of vegetables are finished, they often go hungry."[52] However, although Tao-chi often grieved and complained in his poems, he never despaired of life, since the hardships he suffered were more than compensated for by the beauty he saw in the world around him. Ch'an Buddhism had taught him self-discipline, and he became all but immune to the threats posed by hardship. In a painting dated 1663, Tao-chi's fellow Ch'an priest and painter, K'un-ts'an, explained the chief lesson of Ch'an, i.e., the fortification of one's self: "Buddha was not a lazy fellow. . . . Neither were the Bodhisattvas, nor the sages and kings, Laotze, Chuangtze, and Confucius. It is because the world today is so full of lazy fellows that families have fallen into disorder, the nation has fallen into disorder, and religious establishments have fallen into disorder. In the words of *The Book of Changes*, 'If Heaven's way is to succeed, everyone must continually strengthen himself, without a moment's indolence [*tzu-chiang pu-hsi*].' "[53]

On these pages the artist's calligraphic brushstrokes again play against those of the painting. In turn, both calligraphy and painting, in describing the misty and rippling effects of river water in the evening, heighten the poem's plaintive tone. As if to increase the emotion of these leaves, the calligraphy affects the Huang T'ing-chien (late Northern Sung) style of throbbing brushstrokes, as well as irregular and asymmetrical characters. The calligraphy page is signed "Shih-t'ao Chi," upon which a rectangular intaglio seal is placed: *Tou-pai i-jan pu-shih-tzu* ("my hair is white and I am still illiterate"). On the painting, the pair of square name seals *Yüan-chi* and *Shih-t'ao* again neatly complete the simple composition.

荒亭寂寂荒山裏　老樹垂

谷傍城塹飯後歸誰

山下瓷若條斜暉

8

Chrysanthemums

*Plum blossoms in October
 Sending forth a cold
 fragrance,
Are accompanied by the
 late-bloomer, the
 chrysanthemum;
Since Heaven and Earth
 have no special favorites,
Will the plum and
 the chrysanthemum
 blossom together
 again in the Spring?*

The chrysanthemum, the favorite flower of the best-known ancient recluse-poet T'ao Ch'ien, was the symbol of reclusion (in another Tao-chi album of this period, now in the Sackler Collection at The Art Museum, Princeton University, T'ao Ch'ien smells a chrysanthemum).[54] As Tao-chi prepared to retire, he thought of T'ao Ch'ien, just as countless retired poets and painters had before him, and as others would in the centuries to follow.

Although this poem was written to commemorate an unusual event, the blossoming of plum trees in October, its real subject is the chrysanthemum, which as the perennial late-bloomer symbolizes not only reclusion in itself, but also endurance and integrity, qualities with which the poet would obviously like to identify himself. As his wintry years approached, would there be a second spring, as it were, for the aging artist? The poet's tone is wistfully ironic.

The calligraphy reverts to the gently nostalgic Chung Yu mode of Leaf 1. It is signed "Hsia-tsun-che Yüan-chi" ("the blind arhat, Yüan-chi"), followed by the oval seal K'u-kua-ho-shang Chi hua-fa ("painting method of the Monk of Bitter Melon, Chi"). In the lower right-hand corner of the painting, we find the same rectangular intaglio seal seen on the preceding calligraphy page: "my hair is white and I am still illiterate."

九月寒香露太真東籬曉

節可為隣從來天地無私

運梅菊同開一樣春 九月梅老

暗尊者原濟

9

Late Spring
On the
Mountain

New bamboo shoots grow taller
than the eaves of the house,
Deep in the morning mist,
a mountain peak can be seen;
May in the mountains feels
like November,
Leaning on a railing,
I feel the cold dew
on my coat and hat.

This poem may have been written in the 1670s, when Tao-chi was living in the Anhwei mountains.[55] Although the painting does not illustrate the poem, it does reflect the poet's feelings perfectly: the bare branches seem to be awakening, and the inkwash enveloping the lonely figure makes the damp and chilly mountain almost palpable. This is one of those quiet, almost desultory moments in which our senses are most alert and receptive to the atmosphere around us.

The painting, which is built up with a series of single brush-lines of increasing thickness and intensity, is a perfect illustration of what Tao-chi meant, in his tract on painting, by *i-hua*, "single-stroke painting." The tiny, spidery calligraphy in the Chung Yu manner suits the contemplative mood of the painting. It is signed, "Ch'ing-hsiang Hsiao-ch'eng-k'o Chi" ("follower of Hinayana from Ch'ing-hsiang, Chi"), followed by the small rectangular intaglio seal *Shih-t'ao*, seen earlier on Leaf 1. A complete set of these small seals, reading *Shih-t'ao* and *Yüan-chi*, appears at the tip of the tree branches.

新長龍絲過屋簷曉雲溪處露
峰尖山中四月如十月衣帽憑欄
泠翠霑

清湘小乘客濟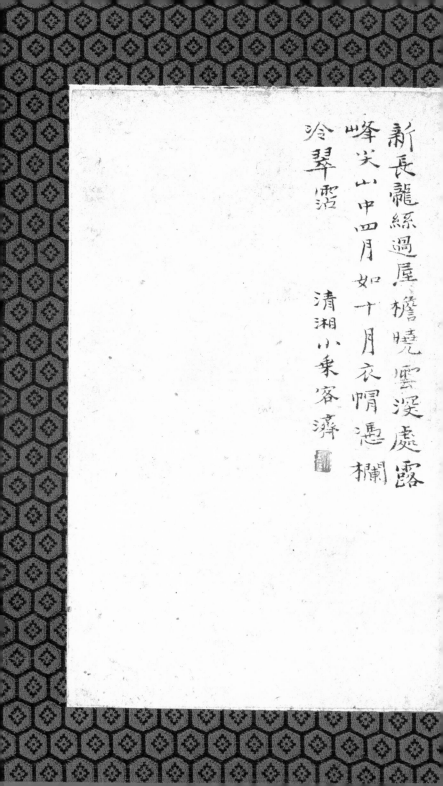

10

Bamboo and Dry Branches

*In this picture I follow
Li Ch'eng's style of branches
with a new idea:
I see a beautiful maiden,
simple and elegant,
with only a touch of cosmetics.
As I try to capture
her inimitable smile,
I suddenly realize that I
shall never entirely succeed.*

Tung Ch'i-ch'ang (1555–1636), in formulating the Orthodox "Southern School" theory of painting, wrote: "Some say, 'One should establish one's own style.' But this cannot be. For example . . . when painting dry branches, one should always follow Li Ch'eng. A thousand years cannot change this. Even if a painter should make his own modifications, he cannot depart from the source. How can anyone put aside the ancient methods and start out on his own?"[56]

In a colophon dated 1686, Tao-chi wrote: "In painting, there are the Southern and the Northern schools, and in calligraphy, the methods of the Two Wangs [Wang Hsi-chih and Hsien-chih]. Chang Jung [fifth century] once remarked, 'I regret not that I do not share the Two Wangs's methods, but that the Two Wangs did not share my methods.' If someone asks whether I [Tao-chi] follow the Southern or the Northern School, or whether either school follows me, I hold my belly laughing and reply, 'I always use my own method!' "[57] Thus Tao-chi makes it quite clear that his real model is nature—the swaying branches that look to him like a "beautiful maiden"—even though he invokes the name of Li Ch'eng.

The accompanying calligraphy, a more elegant version of the Ni Tsan manner, with elements of the style of the T'ang master Li Yung, has the same gaiety and charm as the painting. The calligraphy page is simply signed "Chi," followed by the square intaglio seal *Shih Yüan-chi yin*. The painting is stamped with the pair of name seals *Yüan-chi* and *Shih-t'ao* seen on the other album leaves.

此幀擬李營丘而有別意美人
素質澹妝流麗漫爾效顰
不免氣細　濟

11

Autumn Mountain

The mountain colors are
a hoary green, the trees
are turning autumnal,
A yellowish mist rises thinly
against a rushing stream;
In a traveler's lodge,
Bitter Melon [Tao-chi] passes
his time with a brush,
His painting method ought
to put old Kuan-hsiu to
shame.

Kuan-hsiu (832–912) was a wandering poet-painter-priest of the war-filled Five Dynasties period. His life had been very much like Tao-chi's, and he once summed up his experiences in two lines:

A single water bottle, accompanied by an alms bowl,
together we grow older and older,
A thousand mountains and ten thousand waters have
gone past, again and again.[58]

This is the only landscape in the album to be fully colored in rust and green (the mountain color of the poem). Despite its small size, the scenery appears truly monumental. Brushstrokes—rock outlines, texture strokes, a running stream, foliage patterns, and "moss dots"—crisscross each other, building and expanding until the whole turns into a powerful, flowing design of undulating forces and counterforces.

In turning his works into abstract designs of brushstrokes and compositional movements, Tao-chi reflected a major seventeenth-century development: Wang Yüan-ch'i (1641–1715), an Orthodox master, explained that in painting, "one need pay attention only to the 'breath force' and the general outlines of the design. It is not necessary to represent beautiful scenery, nor is it important to follow old compositions. . . ."[59] In Tao-chi's works, however, nature always remained the source of his inspiration: "Mountains and rivers compel me to speak for them; they are transformed through me and I am transformed through them."[60] In several large compositions, datable to the late 1690s, Tao-chi's seal spells out his painting method: "I search out all of nature's extraordinary peaks to be my designs" (*sou-chin ch'i-feng ta-ts'ao-kao*).[61]

To enhance the hoary and monumental quality of this landscape, the archaic "clerical" script is used. This style of writing, with its severe horizontals and verticals relieved only by flaring slanting strokes, is suitable for formal commemorative inscriptions carved in stone. The calligraphy is signed "Hsia-tsun-che Yüan-chi" ("the blind arhat, Yüan-chi"), over which the square intaglio seal reads *K'u-kua ho-shang* ("Monk of Bitter Melon"). The square name seals *Yüan-chi* and *Shih-t'ao* appear on the right side of the painting.

山色峯〻樹色丹黃雲欲

碎折黏流苦瓜密含消開

筆畫瀘應㥄苦貫休

12

Narcissus

Oh narcissus and plum
blossoms,
you are enjoyed together by
us,
In the wintry months, the two
of you compete for glory;
On a warm day
by a bright window,
I hold my brush,
How my quiet thoughts wander
—beyond the boundless
shores.

The symbolism of the narcissus (*shui-hsien* or "water goddess") entered Chinese thought relatively late and was not fully developed until the late Northern Sung period. In the late thirteenth century, the Southern Sung scholar-painter, and member of the Sung imperial clan, Chao Meng-chien (1199–1267?), popularized it in painting.[62]

The mood of this last poem is comfortably relaxed. Tao-chi was fifty-four years old when these album leaves were executed, and he could enjoy observing a narcissus plant in his study and letting his thoughts "wander—beyond the boundless shores." In dramatizing the personal tragedies of the late-Ming Loyalist painters, later poets often pictured them in flights of sorrow: Cheng Hsieh

(1693–1765), for instance, wrote of K'un-ts'an, Chu Ta, and Tao-chi:

> *Their nation toppled, their families scattered,*
>   *How their temples had turned white,*
> *With a bag full of poems and paintings,*
>   *Each of them became a priest;*
> *Horizontal and vertical,*
>   *Thousands of scrolls they smeared,*
> *How their inkdots were outnumbered by their teardrops!*[63]

But uncontrolled grief has never been the stuff from which great art is made. For Tao-chi, though his nation had toppled, his cultural heritage—flowers, mountains, words, and images—had survived and gained renewed vigor through his brush.

The single narcissus plant on this leaf, though simply done, embodies several brilliant innovations: a faint background wash around the "blank outline," which makes the leaves and blossoms stand out in relief, and the dark and sharp ink strokes accenting the tips of the blossom petals, which are allowed to bleed and thus create a coloristic effect. The simple composition captures wonderfully the fresh vigor of a narcissus in full bloom.

The calligraphy, in a free and bold manner, combines all of Tao-chi's favorite idiosyncrasies—wavering strokes, "clerical" flaring endings, deliberately blunt strokes with firmly centered "hidden" brushtip, and irregular compositions—into a highly individual style. It is carried out with as much ease and self-assurance as the simple drawing of the narcissus. The calligraphy is signed "Hsiao-ch'eng-k'o Chi" ("follower of Hinayana, Chi") and is followed by the rectangular intaglio seal reading, "my hair is white and I am still illiterate"; the painting is accompanied by the double name seals *Yüan-chi* and *Shih-t'ao*.

君点梅苔同賞歲寒
時許草諤暖日清臒
拈筆戲巴清思疊
渾　秉客濟

Colophon by

TOMIOKA TESSAI

(1837-1924)

In a colophon at the end of the album, Tomioka Tessai,[64] Japan's last great Nanga ("Southern School Painting") master and an admirer of Tao-chi, transcribes a commentary by Cheng Hsieh (1693–1765):

> Shih-t'ao, who excelled in painting, was able to paint in a myriad of different ways; orchids and bamboo were easy for him. I, Pan-ch'iao [Cheng Hsieh], can paint only orchids and bamboo. I am over fifty of age, and I paint nothing else. If he [Tao-chi] concentrated on being broad, then I have concentrated on being specialized. And who can say that one is better than the other? Shih-t'ao's painting methods have thousands and tens of thousands of transformations; they can be extraordinarily hoary and ancient, and yet delicate and smooth. Compared to the works of Pa-ta-shan-jen, they show only strengths rather than weaknesses. Today, however, Pa-ta's reputation fills the nation, while Shih-t'ao is known only in our Yangchow prefecture. Why is this so? It is because while Pa-ta uses only one type of reduced brushwork, Shih-t'ao's paintings, by comparison, seem too detailed and luxuriant. Furthermore, Pa-ta is not known by other names; so he is easily remembered. Shih-t'ao, on the other hand, is known not only as Hung-chi, but also as Ch'ing-hsiang-tao-jen, as K'u-hua-ho-shang, as Ta-ti-tzu, and as Hsia-tsun-che. When too many sobriquets are used, they become confusing. Pa-ta is only Pa-ta. Likewise, I, Pan-ch'iao, am always Pan-ch'iao. So, on this account alone, I regret I shall not be following Master Shih [-t'ao].[65]

Around 1900, the album was in the collection of the well-known Japanese collector Kuwana Tetsujō (1864–1938). (A letter by the calligrapher Kusakabe Tōsaku, addressed to Kuwana, postmarked September 7, 1900, is now kept in the box containing the album.) The title, *K'u-kua ho-shang shu-hua-tse* ("Album of Calligraphy and Painting by the Monk of Bitter Melon [Tao-chi]"), written by Mr. Kuwana on the wooden box containing the album, is reproduced here on the slipcase; the cartouche *Shih-t'ao tao-jen shu-hua shen-p'in* ("The Taoist Shih-t'ao's Calligraphy and Painting, Divine Class"), also in Mr. Kuwana's handwriting, is reproduced on the cover of the book.

The album was first published in Hashimoto Kansetsu, *Sekitō* (Tokyo, 1926), plates 13–24. It is also described and fully illustrated in black and white in Edwards, ed., *The Painting of Tao-chi*, pages 42–43 and 111–116.

Notes

1. Followers of Tung Ch'i-ch'ang's (1555–1636) theory of *ta-ch'eng*, the "Great Synthesis," which was based on study of the works of the ancient masters, are known as Orthodox painters, while those painters who developed a personal style are called Individualists.

2. David Hawkes, *A Little Primer of Tu Fu* (Oxford, 1967), pp. 49, 55 (I have modified Professor Hawkes's translation).

3. *Ibid.*, pp. 45, 48.

4. See Wen Fong, *Summer Mountains: The Timeless Landscape* (New York, 1975).

5. See Wen Fong, *Sung and Yuan Paintings* (New York, 1973), p. 71; Sherman E. Lee and Wai-kam Ho, *Chinese Art under the Mongols: The Yüan Dynasty (1279–1368)* (Cleveland, Ohio, 1968), number 236.

6. Some of the principal biographical sources are Fu Pao-shih, *Shih-t'ao shang-jen nien-p'u (Chronology of Shih-t'ao)* (Shanghai, 1948); Wen Fong, "A Letter from Shih-t'ao to Pa-ta-shan-jen and the Problem of Shih-t'ao's Chronology," *Archives of the Chinese Art Society of America,* XIII (1959), pp. 22–53; Cheng Cho-lu, *Shih-t'ao yen-chiu (A Study of Shih-t'ao)* (Peking, 1961), reprinted in *Chung-kuo ming-hua-chia ts'ung-shu* (Hong Kong, 1970), vol. 2; Cheng Wei, "Lun Shih-t'ao sheng-huo, hsing-ching, ssu-hsiang ti-pien chi i-shu ch'eng-chiu" ("On Shih-t'ao's Life, Intellectual Development, and Artistic Achievement"), *Wen-wu,* number 12 (1962), pp. 6–7, 43–50; Richard Edwards, ed., *The Painting of Tao-chi: Catalogue of an Exhibition, August 13–September 17, 1967* (Ann Arbor, Michigan, 1967); Li Yeh-shuang, *Shih-t'ao ti Shih-chieh (Shih-t'ao and His World)* (Taipei, 1973); Marilyn Fu and Shen Fu, *Studies in Connoisseurship: Chinese Paintings from the Arthur M. Sackler Collection in New York and Princeton* (Princeton, 1973) (this last includes a full bibliography on Tao-chi and a summary of the problem of establishing his birth date). Ming-fu, "Shih-t'ao Yüan-chi ch'an-shih hsing-shih k'ao ("Studies on Life of Ch'an master Shih-t'ao Yüan-chi"), *I-t'ai* (Taipei, 1974-76), vols. 79–95, in thirteen installments.

7. Fu Pao-shih, *Shih-t'ao shang-jen nien-p'u,* p. 65.

8. They were Hsiung K'ai-yüan and Chang Yu-yü; see *Chung-kuo ming-hua-chia ts'ung-shu* (Hong Kong, 1970), vol. 2, under "K'un-ts'an," pp. 1173–74.

9. I-ting, "*Po-yu-chi* tso-che Mu-ch'en Min" ("Mu-ch'en Min, Author of the *Collection of the Northern Journey*"), *I-lin ts'ung-lu* (Hong Kong, 1962), vol. 3, pp. 146–50; Hsü Fu-kuan, *Shih-t'ao chih i-yen-chiu (Another Study of Shih-t'ao)* (Taipei, 1973), pp. 99–103.

10. The inscription, a specimen of Tao-chi's early handwriting, is reproduced in Fu and Fu, *Studies in Connoisseurship*, p. 36.

11. Fu Pao-shih, *Shih-t'ao shang-jen nien-p'u*, pp. 64–65. A handscroll showing the two poems describing his audiences with K'ang-hsi is in the collection of The Art Museum at Princeton University.

12. *Ibid.*, p. 56.

13. *Ibid.*, pp. 65–66.

14. *Ibid.*, p. 45.

15. Li Yeh-shuang, *Shih-t'ao ti shih-chieh*, p. 20.

16. Fu Pao-shih, *Shih-t'ao shang-jen nien-p'u*, p. 66.

17. *Ibid.*, p. 68. This poem is transcribed by Tao-chi in his well-known handscroll *Sketches of Calligraphy and Painting by Ch'ing-hsiang*, dated in the autumn of 1696, now in Peking; for the scroll see *Ch'ing-hsiang shu-hua-kao chüan* (Peking, 1961).

18. Fu Pao-shih, *op. cit.*, p. 70; *see also Ch'ing-hsiang shu-hua-kao chüan.*

19. *Ibid.*

20. The exact date of his death is not known. For a discussion of this problem, see Cheng Wei, "Kuan-hsi Shih-t'ao tsu-nien ti wan-ch'i tso-p'in" ("On Some of Shin-t'ao's Late Works that Bear upon His Death Date"), *I-lin ts'ung-lu* (Hong Kong, 1973), vol. 8, pp. 160–67.

21. The final section of the *Sketches of Calligraphy and Painting by Ch'ing-hsiang* scroll shows a "blind arhat" in a hollow tree trunk; see Edwards, ed., *The Painting of Tao-chi*, p. 41, fig. 18.

22. See Lee and Ho, *Chinese Art under the Mongols*, p. 95.

23. Fong, "A Letter from Shih-t'ao," p. 28.

24. For the most recent detailed discussion of this incident, see Yeh-yeh, "Lun 'Hu I-t'ang shih-pien' chi-ch'i tui Pa-ta-shan-jen ti ying-hsiang" ("On the Hu I-t'ang Incident and Its Effect on Pa-ta-shan-jen"), *Ta-lu tsa-chih* (Taipei, 1975), vol. 51, number 6, pp. 257–81.

25. Fong, "A Letter from Shih-t'ao," p. 27. A version of this long inscription (possibly a copy) is reproduced in Fu and Fu, *Studies in Connoisseurship*, p. 210, fig. 11.

26. Marilyn Fu and Wen Fong, *The Wilderness Colors of Tao-chi* (New York, 1973), number 8.

27. Edwards, ed., *The Painting of Tao-chi*, p. 61, under 1707; also Fu and Fu, *Studies in Connoisseurship*, number 34, pp. 302–13.

28. See Fu Pao-shih, *Shih-t'ao shang-jen nien-p'u*, p. 79.

29. See the poem on plum blossom on Leaf 9 in an album dated 1695, recorded in *ibid.*, p. 76.

30. *Ibid.*, p. 77.

31. Yüan T'ung, "Shih Shih-ch'i shih-tsi hui-pien" ("Collection of Writings about Shih-ch'i"), first published in about 1940, reprinted in *Kou-tao-jen i-chu, Chung-ho yüeh-k'an lun-wen hsüan-chi* (Taipei, 1975), vol. 1, p. 314.

32. Fu Pao-shih, *Shih-t'ao shang-jen pien-p'u*, p. 54. The same inscription appears on a hanging scroll at the Musée Guimet, Paris, which is dated autumn of 1671; see Edwards, ed., *The Painting of Tao-chi*, pp. 74, 100.

33. Fu Pao-shih, *op. cit.*, p. 41; Li Yeh-shuang, *Shih-t'ao ti shih-chieh*, p. 26.

34. These scrolls and albums are predominantly in the linear, "blank-outline" style. The painter's writings on the album leaves are also more or less uniform in style.

35. Yüan T'ung, "Shih Shih-ch'i," p. 228.

36. See Fu and Fu, *Studies in Connoisseurship*, pp. 52–53.

37. Beginning with the album of 1682 (formerly in the Chang Dai-chien collection, reproduced in *Ta-feng-t'ang ming-chi* [*Masterpieces of Chinese Painting from the Great Wind Hall Collection*] [Kyoto, 1955–56], plates 24–28), the linear, "blank-outline" drawing is used more and more in combination with inkwashes that model and complete the "blank-outline" forms; the individual leaves of the album also show an increasing range of styles—wet or dry, full or sparse. At the same time, the painter's writing styles begin to vary, in a carefully planned manner, from one leaf to the next.

38. Roderick Whitfield, with an addendum by Wen Fong, *In Pursuit of Antiquity* (Princeton, 1969).

39. A free English translation of the entire text is in Lin Yu-tang, *The Chinese Theory of Art* (London, 1967). The original text appears in *Hua-lun-ts'ung-k'an (Anthology of Painting Theories)* (Peking, 1960), vol. 1.

40. Cheng Cho-lu, *Shih-t'ao yen-chiu*, pp. 49–50.

41. Tao-chi, *Hua-yü-lu*, chs. 1, "On *i-hua*," and 7, "On *yin-yün*."

42. See Kung Hsien's Sketchbook, datable to the 1680s, reproduced in *Shina-nanga-taisei* (*Anthology of Chinese Southern School Paintings*) (Tokyo, 1935–37), suppl. vol. 3, p. 255.

43. See Cheng Cho-lu, *Shih-t'ao yen-chiu*, pp. 70–71.

44. See *Chih-pu-tsu-chai ts'ung-shu* (Taipei, n.d.), vol. 9, p. 5,673.

45. Some of the better-known examples are Leaf 7 of a small album of twelve leaves depicting the scenery of Huang-shan, dated about 1696, in the Kanichi Sumitomo collection, Oiso; the handscroll *View of Huang-shan*, dated 1699, also in the Sumitomo collection; a large hanging scroll entitled *Thirty-six Peaks of Huang-shan Recollected*, about 1700, in The Metropolitan Museum of Art; and Leaf 1 of an album of ten leaves, dated 1701, in the Arthur M. Sackler collection at The Art Museum, Princeton University.

46. *Ta-ti-tzu t'i-hua shih-pa* (*Tao-chi's Poetic Colophons*), in *Mei-shu ts'ung-shu* (Shanghai, 1928), vol. 15/2/53-4.

47. David Hawkes, *Ch'u Tz'u: The Songs of the South* (London, 1950), p. 76.

48. Hsia Wen-yen, *T'u-hui pao-chien*, ch. 5.

49. T'ao Ch'ien (T'ao Yüan-ming) told the famous story that during the T'ai-yüan era (376-396), a fisherman of Wu-ling lost his way and found himself in a never-never land of peach blossoms where he met villagers whose ancestors had escaped there during the war years of the Ch'in period, in the third century B.C. See Herbert A. Giles, *A History of Chinese Literature* (New York, 1958), pp. 130–31.

50. Fu Pao-shih, *Shih-t'ao shang-jen nien-p'u*, pp. 77-78.

51. Giles, *A History of Chinese Literature*, p. 219.

52. Fu Pao-shih, *Shih-t'ao Shang-jen nien-p'u*, p. 52.

53. Yüan T'ung, "Shih Shih-ch'i," p. 211. The painting, *The Pao-en Temple*, dated 1664, is in the Sumitomo collection, Oiso; see Osvald Sirén, *Chinese Painting: Leading Masters and Principles* (London, 1958), vol. 6, plate 374.

54. Fu and Fu, *Studies in Connoisseurship*, p. 192.

55. Fu Pao-shih, *Shih-t'ao shang-jen nien-p'u*, p. 51, under 1674.

56. Tung Ch'i-ch'ang, *Hua ch'an-shih sui-pi*, 2/2b–3a.

57. Tao-chi's colophon dated 1686 appears on his hanging scroll *View of Huang-shan*, painted in 1667; see Fu and Fu, *Studies in Connoisseurship*, p. 56. In 1686 Tao-chi was in Nanking. It is possible that he had knowledge of Chang I's statement, quoted above, which was found on a painting of the 1660s by K'un-ts'an (who also worked in Nanking); see above, note 35.

58. Kuan-hsiu, *Ch'an-yüeh-chi, in Li-tai hua-chia shih-wen-chi (Collection of Poems and Writings by Painters)* (Taipei, 1975), vol. 20, p. 437.

59. Whitfield, *In Pursuit of Antiquity*, p. 184.

60. Tao-chi, *Hua-yü lu*, ch. 8, "On Mountains and Rivers."

61. The phrase is also found in Tao-chi, *Hua-yü lu*, ch. 8.

62. Wen Fong, *Sung and Yuan Paintings*, pp. 68–71.

63. Cheng Hsieh, *Pan-chi'iao-chi* (Shanghai, 1933), p. 73.

64. For an account of his life and art, see Taro Odakane, *Tessai: Master of the Literati Style*, trans. and adapted by Money Hickman (Tokyo and Rutland, Vt., 1965).

65. Cheng Hsieh, *Pan-ch'iao-chi*, pp. 13–14.